SO-GOOD MEALS

Better Homes and Gardens

MEREDITH PRESS

BETTER HOMES AND GARDENS CREATIVE COOKING LIBRARY, FIRST PRINTING

Contents

This seal means recipe goodness!

Every recipe in this book is *endorsed* by Better Homes & Gardens Test Kitchen. Each food was tested over and over till it rated superior—in practicality, ease of prep-aration, and deliciousness.

Meals men like

Fix any of these delicious meals for your man and you'll be the "Best Cook" he knows. Here are old-time favorites that offer mighty good eating—from thick broiled burgers to standing rib roast and savory brown stew!

Crisp Cabbage Slaw

2 cups shredded new cabbage
½ cup *each* diced cucumber and celery
¼ cup chopped green pepper
1 teaspoon salt
¼ teaspoon paprika
½ cup salad dressing
2 tablespoons vinegar
1 teaspoon prepared mustard

Combine chilled vegetables, salt, and paprika. Combine remaining ingredients; pour over. Toss lightly. Trim with pimiento.

Apple Betty Pie

Apple crisp baked like a deep-dish pie. Flavor flair is fresh orange—

4 cups sliced pared tart apples or
    1 No. 2 can (2½ cups) sliced
    apples, drained
¼ cup orange juice
         • • •
1 cup sugar
¾ cup all-purpose flour
½ teaspoon cinnamon
¼ teaspoon nutmeg
Dash salt
½ cup butter or margarine

Mound apples in buttered 9-inch pie plate; sprinkle with orange juice. For topping, combine sugar, flour, spices and salt; cut in butter until mixture is crumbly; then scatter over apples.

Bake in moderate oven (375°) 45 minutes or until apples are done and topping is crisp and lightly browned. Trim with twisted orange slices tacked with cloves. Serve warm with pitcher of light cream or scoops of vanilla ice cream. Serves 6.

1 It's the browning that gives a stew the rich color and flavor men like. Heat fat in Dutch oven. Add beef chuck; brown on all sides—turn cubes with tongs. This should take about 20 minutes. Add sliced onion, along with garlic (on toothpick so you can retrieve it!), boiling water, salt, lemon juice, sugar, Worcestershire sauce, pepper, paprika, bay leaf, and allspice or cloves.

Old-time Beef Stew

This gravy-rich beef stew calls for soup bowls— and spoons as well as forks so as not to waste even a drop!—

2 tablespoons fat
2 pounds beef chuck, cut in
   1½-inch cubes
1 large onion, sliced
1 clove garlic
4 cups boiling water
1 tablespoon salt
1 tablespoon lemon juice
1 teaspoon sugar
1 teaspoon Worcestershire sauce
½ teaspoon pepper
½ teaspoon paprika
1 or 2 bay leaves
Dash allspice or cloves
6 carrots, cut in quarters
1 pound small white onions
6 medium potatoes, diced (optional)
½ cup cold water
¼ cup flour

Follow the directions under the pictures.

2 Gentle cooking is what makes the meat tender, so cover and simmer (not boil), 2 hours. (Stir now and then to prevent sticking.) When meat is almost done, add the vegetables. For handsome look, cut each kind of vegetable in same-size pieces—note bias-cut carrots in the picture. Now simmer the stew about 30 minutes longer or till everything in the kettle is tender. Discard the bay leaf and garlic clove.

3 Gravy time. Pour cold water into a shaker then add flour; shake hard to blend. Remove from heat, push the meat and vegetables to one side of the pan; stir in flour mixture. Cook, stirring constantly, till the gravy thickens and boils. Cook gently about 5 minutes more. No lumps!

This stew will serve 6 to 8 hungry folks. Serve while piping hot. Go-withs are creamy slaw and thick slices of bread.

Chicken Garden Skillet

¼ cup fat
1 2½- to 3-pound ready-to-cook
   broiler-fryer chicken, cut up
Seasoned flour
¾ cup chicken broth
¾ cup cooking sherry

•   •   •

1 package frozen artichoke hearts
2 tomatoes, cut in wedges
1 medium onion, sliced
½ medium green pepper, sliced

In skillet, melt fat (at 360°, if using electric skillet). Meanwhile, dredge chicken pieces in seasoned flour. Brown slowly in the hot fat, turning once.

Reduce heat (or reduce temperature of electric skillet to 230°); add broth and cooking sherry to chicken; cover, cook 45 minutes.

Add vegetables; sprinkle with salt. Cover; cook just till artichokes are done, about 15 minutes. Makes 4 servings.

Toasted Cheese Loaf

Crusty "rolls," pillow-soft inside—

Cut crusts from top and sides of 1 unsliced sandwich loaf, about 11 inches long. Make 8 slices crosswise, cutting to, *but not through*, bottom crust. Make one cut lengthwise down the center. Place on baking sheet.

Blend ½ cup butter or margarine and two 5-ounce jars sharp spreading cheese. Spread between slices, over top and sides.

Tie string around loaf to hold together. Bake in hot oven (400°) until cheese is melted and bread is crusty, about 15 minutes. Serve like pan rolls. Makes 16.

Zesty Ripe Olives

Drain one 7-ounce can pitted ripe olives; place in jar. Pour ½ cup clear French dressing over olives; add one clove garlic, minced. Cover jar tightly. Invert jar several times to coat olives with dressing. Chill 6 hours or overnight. To serve, drain olives; spear on toothpicks.

Pineapple Sherbet

½ envelope (1½ teaspoons)
   unflavored gelatin
2 tablespoons cold water
2 cups buttermilk
¾ cup sugar
1 9-ounce can (1 cup) crushed
   pineapple
1 teaspoon vanilla
1 egg white
¼ cup sugar

Soften gelatin in cold water; dissolve over hot water. Combine buttermilk with next three ingredients and gelatin; mix well. Freeze in refrigerator tray till firm.

Break in chunks; turn into chilled bowl; beat smooth with electric or rotary beater. Beat egg white till soft peaks form; gradually add ¼ cup sugar, beating to stiff peaks. Fold into pineapple mixture. Return to *cold* tray. Freeze firm.

Coconut-Oatmeal Cookies

2 cups quick-cooking rolled oats
⅔ cup flaked coconut
1 cup butter or margarine
1 cup sugar
2 eggs
3 tablespoons milk
1½ teaspoons vanilla
1½ cups sifted all-purpose flour
½ teaspoon *each* soda and salt

In oven, toast oats and coconut till golden brown. Thoroughly cream butter and sugar; add eggs, milk, and vanilla; beat well. Sift together dry ingredients; add to creamed mixture, blend well. Stir in oats and coconut. Drop from teaspoon, 2 inches apart, on ungreased cooky sheet. Flatten with tumbler dipped in sugar.

Bake at 400° for 8 to 10 minutes or till lightly browned. Remove at once from pan; cool. Makes 4 dozen.

Veal Bird Feast

Veal Birds   Brown Gravy
Parsleyed Carrots
Buttered New Potatoes
Pineapple Emerald Ring
Fan-tan Rolls   Raspberry Jam
Sponge Cake with
Lemon Cream
Coffee or Tea

Long-time favorite

Veal Birds are as homey and delicious now as when they reached popularity at the turn of the century.

Veal Birds

2 pounds veal round steak,
   ½ inch thick
1½ cups finely diced dry bread cubes
2 tablespoons butter, melted
3 tablespoons finely chopped onion
1 teaspoon sage
¼ teaspoon salt
1 teaspoon water

Cut meat into 6 pieces; pound till double in area (¼-inch thick). Sprinkle lightly with salt and pepper. For stuffing, sprinkle bread cubes with remaining ingredients; toss lightly. Top each piece of meat with stuffing and roll up lightly as for jelly roll; tie loosely with string.

Sprinkle with salt and pepper. Roll in flour. Brown veal rolls nicely on all sides in ⅓ cup butter. Add ½ cup water. Simmer, covered, 30 minutes or till tender. Remove birds to platter; keep warm.

Gravy: Pour pan drippings into a pint measure. Spoon fat (about 3 tablespoons) back into skillet; add 3 tablespoons all-purpose flour. Brown flour well, stirring constantly. Remove from heat.

Add water to meat juices to make 1¾ cups; stir into flour mixture. Add ½ teaspoon monosodium glutamate and 1 teaspoon concentrated meat extract. Cook and stir till mixture thickens and boils. Add salt and pepper to taste; simmer 1 minute.

Pineapple Emerald Ring

2 3-ounce packages lime-flavored
   gelatin
2 cups hot water
3 No. 1 flat cans pineapple slices
3 tablespoons lemon juice
1½ cups green seedless grapes

Dissolve gelatin in hot water; add dash salt. Drain pineapple, reserving syrup. Add lemon juice to pineapple syrup, then add enough cold water to make 2 cups. Add syrup mixture to gelatin; and chill till mixture is partially set.

Arrange pineapple slices on edge, two together, at 6 intervals around 6½-cup ring mold. Place grapes between pineapple dividers. Pour gelatin over. Chill firm.

If the pineapple slices extend above gelatin, trim before unmolding.

Lemon Cream

Mix 1 cup sugar, 2 tablespoons all-purpose flour, dash salt, ¾ cup water; blend in ¼ cup lemon juice, and 1 slightly beaten egg. Heat quickly to boiling, stirring constantly; cook and stir 1 minute. Cover; cool to room temperature.

Fold in ½ cup whipping cream, whipped, and ½ teaspoon grated lemon peel. Chill. Serve as sauce on wedges of angel cake or squares of white cake. Makes 2¼ cups.

It's Burger Night!

Betterburgers

Onion Slices   Burger Relishes

Toasty Garlic Slices

Tossed Green Salad

Fudge Sundaes

or Apple-Nut Squares

Coffee   Cream and Sugar

Betterburgers

Pan-broiled: See directions under the pictures below.

Broiled: If desired, cook ½ cup chopped onion in small amount hot fat till tender but not brown. Combine 1 pound ground beef, 1 teaspoon salt, dash pepper, and the onion. Form burgers, using ½- or ⅓-cup measure. Broil 3 inches from heat about 6 minutes; turn and broil 6 minutes more or till done to your liking. Serve on warm buttered buns with relishes.

Helps for burger makers

• If beef is lean, have 2 or 3 ounces suet ground with each pound. Burgers will be more moist and tender. Medium or coarsely ground meat is best.

• Kid-glove handling helps to keep burgers light. In shaping patties by hand, pat rather than spank. And don't overcook!

• For same-size burgers, slice from a roll, as shown below. Or fill a ⅓- or ½-cup measure with meat for each patty.

• Flip only once—if you turn the patties more than that, they are likely to mash down, be less airy.

• When making burgers for a crowd, stack them up—put wax paper between each.

• If burgers need to wait a few minutes after cooking, here's a way to keep them piping hot, extra juicy. While burgers broil, heat equal amount of butter or margarine and Worcestershire sauce—enough to coat burgers. When patties are done to your liking, transfer to sauce in the hot skillet, turning once.

For juicy Pan-broiled Betterburgers, cook fast in salted skillet

1 Burgers will be juicy and tender every time this no-pack way! Shape your whole package of hamburger in a roll. Do this with a light touch, rolling it on wax paper, under your finger tips. Don't press.

Slice the roll in ½- to ¾-inch slices. Round edges of the patties if you like. Now the burgers are ready to be pan-broiled.

2 Heat skillet sizzling hot. Shake salt into the empty skillet—the same as if you were salting burgers, about ½ to 1 teaspoon. Put the burgers in the pan; sear them on one side only—about 1 minute.

Lower heat, cook a few minutes. Turn burgers, cook 2 or 3 minutes on the second side or until done to your liking. Serve on buns or toast.

***Tender Betterburgers
—almost like steak!*** Serve them upon Toasty Garlic Slices to catch all the good burger juices, and pass go-withs—mustard and catsup, relish, onion slices. This meal rates "super" with Dad and the kids!

Tossed Green Salad

Rub cut end of garlic clove over bowl, or mince clove in garlic press and add to dressing. Break lettuce into bowl by hand, in bite-size pieces—it looks fresher than lettuce cut with a knife.

For a treat, try salads with different greens—tiny heads of Bibb lettuce cut in quarters, tender water cress, curly endive, escarole, or tiny spinach leaves.

Last, toss with dressing. Just before serving, pour on Italian or French dressing, bottled or "home-mixed." Use just enough to coat the greens. Add freshly ground pepper for zip, and a dash salt.

At last minute gently toss in tomato wedges, or other ingredients—like cucumber slices, avocado cubes, olive or radish slices, crisp corn chips. Or, arrange atop greens; add dressing, toss at table.

Toasty Garlic Slices

Melt ⅓ cup butter in 11x7x1½-inch baking dish. Add 1 or 2 cloves garlic, minced. Add six 1-inch slices French bread, turning quickly to butter both sides. Let stand 10 minutes. Heat in 350° oven about 20 minutes.

Fudge Sundaes

2 tablespoons butter
2 1-ounce squares unsweetened chocolate
1 cup sugar
1 6-ounce can (⅔ cup) evaporated milk
1 teaspoon vanilla

Mix butter, chocolate, sugar, evaporated milk in saucepan; cook and stir over medium heat till thick and blended. Remove from heat. Add vanilla. Cool thoroughly. Serve over ice cream.

Apple-Nut Squares

1 beaten egg
¾ cup sugar
½ teaspoon vanilla
½ cup sifted all-purpose flour
¼ teaspoon salt
1 teaspoon baking powder
1 cup chopped unpared tart apples
½ cup broken California walnuts

Combine egg, sugar, and vanilla. Sift together dry ingredients; add to egg mixture and blend well. Stir in apples, and nuts. Spread in greased 8x8x2-inch baking dish.

Bake at 350° for 30 minutes or till done. Cut in squares. Makes 6 servings.

**For festive occasion—
glazed-ham dinner**

Glazed Rolled Ham is easy to carve—no bone. Spiced Peaches and nut-crusted Sweet-potato Balls look like a party, are delicious, too. For contrast—Perfection Salad Mold in a ring.

Come-and-get-it Ham Supper

Glazed Rolled Ham
Mustard Sauce
Sweet-potato Balls
Warm Rolls
Perfection Salad Mold
Honey-Raisin Cheesecake
Coffee

Spiced Peaches

In saucepan combine 1 No. 2½ can (3½ cups) peach halves, 1 tablespoon mixed pickling spices *or* 3 to 6 inches stick cinnamon, 1 teaspoon whole cloves, 1 tablespoon vinegar; heat to boiling. Simmer 5 minutes.

Serve warm if placed on platter with ham; or serve warm or chilled in bowl. Drain before serving. (Save the syrup to use in Marmalade Glaze or simply glaze the ham with the syrup.) Stud peaches with additional whole cloves, if desired.

Glazed Rolled Ham

Buy a boneless and fully cooked ham (the amount depends on the crowd). Place ham on rack in shallow roasting pan. Do not cover or add water. Heat in slow oven (325°) according to directions on wrapper or till meat thermometer reads 130°. Half an hour before time is up, spoon Marmalade Glaze over ham. Continue heating 30 minutes more, spooning glaze over 2 or 3 times.

To roast on spit: Center ham lengthwise on spit (first tie ham with cord if necessary); place in rotisserie. Roast about 10 minutes per pound. Last 30 minutes spoon Marmalade Glaze occasionally over ham.

Marmalade Glaze: To orange marmalade, add enough syrup from Spiced Peaches to make of spooning consistency. For garnish, slice 1 or 2 of the peach halves and peg on the ham with whole cloves.

Mustard Sauce

Combine 1 cup dairy sour cream, 3 tablespoons packaged onion-soup mix, and 1½ to 2 tablespoons prepared mustard. Heat slowly just to bubbling, stirring now and then. Makes about 1 cup.

Sweet-potato Balls

2½ cups mashed canned or cooked sweet potatoes (1 1-pound 2-ounce vacuum can or about 2 pounds fresh)
½ teaspoon salt
Dash pepper
2 tablespoons butter or margarine, melted
⅓ cup honey
1 tablespoon butter or margarine
1 cup chopped pecans

Combine mashed sweet potatoes, salt, pepper, and 2 tablespoons butter; chill for easier handling. Shape in 8 balls. Heat honey and 1 tablespoon butter in small heavy skillet over high heat. When syrup is hot, remove from heat; add potato balls, one at a time. Spoon glaze over, coating completely.

Roll in chopped nuts. Place balls so they do not touch each other in greased shallow baking dish or pan. Bake in moderate oven (350°) 20 to 25 minutes.

Perfection Salad

2 envelopes (2 tablespoons) unflavored gelatin
½ cup sugar
1 teaspoon salt
1½ cups boiling water
1½ cups cold water
½ cup vinegar
2 tablespoons lemon juice
Stuffed green olives, sliced
2 cups finely shredded cabbage
1 cup chopped celery
¼ cup chopped pimiento
½ cup chopped green pepper

Mix gelatin, sugar, and salt. Add boiling water and stir till gelatin is dissolved. Add cold water, vinegar, and lemon juice; chill till partially set. Pour about ½ cup in 6½-cup ring mold. Arrange trios of stuffed-olive slices in mold; chill firm.

Mix remaining partially set gelatin with cabbage, celery, pimiento, and green pepper. Carefully pour over gelatin in mold. Chill till set. Unmold.

Fill center with tiny whole cooked or canned carrots that have been marinated in Italian or French dressing overnight or at least 2 hours. Tuck in few leaves of Bibb lettuce. Platter trim: Stuffed green olives, ripe olives, and pickle slices atop Bibb leaves.

Honey-Raisin Cheesecake

It's a smooth creamy-rich filling topped with toasted almonds—

Butter Crust: Mix 1 cup sifted all-purpose flour, ¼ cup sugar, and ¼ teaspoon salt; cut in ¼ cup butter till mixture resembles coarse crumbs. Blend in 1 slightly beaten egg. Pat dough evenly on bottom and 1 inch up sides of an 8x8x2-inch baking dish. Bake in hot oven (400°) 15 minutes; cool. Sprinkle ½ cup seedless raisins over crust.

Cheese Filling: Beat smooth 3 cups cream-style cottage cheese. Add 4 eggs, one at a time, beating well after each. Add ½ cup honey, ¼ cup sifted all-purpose flour, ¼ cup sugar, 1 teaspoon grated lemon peel, ½ teaspoon vanilla, and ¼ teaspoon salt; blend well. Pour over raisins. Sprinkle top with ¼ cup toasted sliced almonds. Bake in slow oven (325°) 40 minutes or till set. Cut in 9 or 12 squares.

Swiss Steak Supper

Oven-barbecued Swiss Steak *or*
Mushroom Pot Roast
Baked Potatoes with Chives
Buttered Corn
Cabbage-Carrot Salad
Brownie Pudding   Coffee

Meat Tips

Braise less-tender cuts like round steak, pot roast, and short ribs at a lazy bubble (*don't boil*). Brown first—slowly on all sides—to bring out flavor. Rub in seasoned flour ahead if you like. Cook covered.

Oven-barbecued Swiss Steak

2 pounds round or chuck steak,
   1 inch thick
2 8-ounce cans (2 cups) seasoned
   tomato sauce
1 tablespoon sugar
1 tablespoon vinegar
1 tablespoon Worcestershire sauce
2 dashes bottled hot pepper sauce
1 medium onion, sliced

Combine $\frac{1}{3}$ cup all-purpose flour, a teaspoon salt, and $\frac{1}{4}$ teaspoon pepper; coat meat with mixture. Brown *slowly* on both sides in hot fat. Spoon off excess fat.

Combine next 5 ingredients and pour over. Add salt and pepper to taste. Simmer uncovered 5 minutes; add onion slices. Cover and bake in oven-going skillet or Dutch oven at 350° for 1 to $1\frac{1}{4}$ hours or until fork tender. Makes 6 servings.

Make Swiss Steak one of your specialties!

Oven-barbecued Swiss Steak, fork-tender, smothered in onions and a rich tomato-y sauce, makes dinner a big occasion. Round out the meal with Cabbage-Carrot Salad and Buttered Corn.

Beef Swiss Steak—section it, then slice meat across the grain

This is a thick-cut round steak. Divide it into two pieces at the natural seam that goes the length of the steak. Then cut across the meat to remove a piece that is convenient size to carve. Cut in two or three pieces.

Turn one of the pieces on edge and carve it across the grain similar to the way you would carve a pot roast. Repeat the same carving procedure with the other half. Use a sharp knife. This one has a scalloped edge.

Mushroom Pot Roast

3 to 4 pounds beef pot roast
2 onions, sliced
½ cup water
⅓ cup cooking sherry
1 clove garlic, minced
¼ teaspoon *each* mustard,
    marjoram, rosemary, thyme
1 bay leaf
1 6-ounce can broiled sliced
    mushrooms

Trim off excess fat. Dredge meat in flour. Brown slowly on all sides in a little hot fat. Season generously with salt and pepper. Add onions. Mix and add remaining ingredients except mushrooms. Cover; cook slowly 2½ hours or till done.

Add mushrooms (and liquid); heat. Remove meat to warm platter. Skim fat from stock. Blend 1 tablespoon flour and ¼ cup cold water; gradually stir into stock. Cook and stir till sauce thickens; salt to taste. Serve over meat. Serves 6 to 8.

Baked Potatoes

Select uniform baking potatoes (not new potatoes). Scrub with brush. For soft skins, rub with fat. Bake at 425° for 40 to 60 minutes. *Or,* if potatoes share oven, bake at 350° to 375° for 60 to 80 minutes.

When done, roll gently under hand to make mealy. Cut crisscross in top with fork; press ends, push up fluff. Drop in a pat of butter and season.

Foil-baked Potatoes: Scrub, dry, wrap in foil. Bake at 350° about 1½ hours.

Cabbage-Carrot Salad

In a cabbage-leaf-lined bowl, arrange a border of 1½ cups finely shredded red cabbage, then a ring of 1½ cups finely shredded green cabbage; center with 1 cup shredded carrots. (Have vegetables chilled and crisp.)

Toss with Dressing: Mix together ½ cup mayonnaise or salad dressing, 1 tablespoon vinegar, 2 teaspoons sugar, and ¼ teaspoon salt. Makes 6 servings.

Brownie Pudding

1 cup sifted all-purpose flour
¾ cup granulated sugar
2 tablespoons cocoa
2 teaspoons baking powder
½ teaspoon salt
½ cup milk
2 tablespoons salad oil *or*
    melted shortening
1 teaspoon vanilla
¾ to 1 cup chopped walnuts
    • • •
¾ cup brown sugar
¼ cup cocoa
1¾ cups hot water

Sift together first 5 ingredients. Add milk, salad oil, and vanilla; mix till smooth. Stir in nuts. Pour into greased 8x8x2-inch pan. Mix together brown sugar and ¼ cup cocoa; sprinkle over batter. Pour hot water over entire batter. Bake in moderate oven (350°) 45 minutes. Serve while warm. Makes 6 to 8 servings.

The Best Meat Loaf—
an all-time favorite

Juicy and moist, it's a dandy slicer. The savory flavor is a just-right blend of herbs and seasoned tomato sauce. If you have some left over, chill and slice it for sandwiches next day.

Meat Loaf Oven Dinner

Best Meat Loaf
Parmesan Potato Bake
Broccoli Spears   Mustard Sauce
Tomato Wedges
Oven-warmed Rolls
Baked Prune Whip   Custard Sauce

An oven meal gives you time to make go-withs at the last minute.
Mustard Sauce: Combine 1 cup dairy sour cream, 3 tablespoons packaged onion-soup mix, and 1½ to 2 tablespoons prepared mustard. Heat slowly just to bubbling, stirring now and then. Serve with broccoli.

Best Meat Loaf

1½ pounds ground beef
1 cup medium cracker crumbs
2 beaten eggs
1 8-ounce can (1 cup) seasoned
    tomato sauce
½ cup finely chopped green onion
2 tablespoons chopped green pepper
1½ teaspoons salt
1 medium bay leaf, crushed
Dash thyme
Dash marjoram

• • •

Chili sauce

Combine all ingredients except chili sauce; mix well. Shape mixture in a loaf in shallow baking dish. Score the loaf by pressing top with handle of wooden spoon as shown on opposite page. Fill the score marks with chili sauce. Bake in moderate oven (350°) 1 hour. Makes 6 to 8 servings.

Custard Sauce

Combine 4 beaten egg yolks, dash salt, and ¼ cup sugar. Gradually stir in 2 cups milk, scalded and slightly cooled. Cook in double boiler over *hot, not boiling* water, stirring constantly, until mixture coats metal spoon.

Remove from heat; cool at once by placing pan in bowl of cold water and stirring a minute or two. Add 1 teaspoon vanilla. Chill. Makes 2 cups.

Baked Prune Whip

2 cups cooked prunes, drained

• • •

1 teaspoon grated lemon peel
2 teaspoons lemon juice
4 tablespoons confectioners' sugar
Dash salt
4 stiff-beaten egg whites

Pit prunes and mash to a pulp. Blend in lemon peel, juice, 2 *tablespoons* confectioners' sugar, and salt. To beaten egg whites, add remaining confectioners' sugar; beat till stiff. Fold prune mixture into egg whites. Pile lightly into 1½-quart baking dish.

Bake in moderate oven (350°) 20 to 30 minutes or till knife inserted in center comes out clean. Serve warm with Custard Sauce. Makes 6 to 8 servings.

Parmesan Potato Bake

½ package quick hash-brown potatoes
   (enough for 4 servings)
1 can frozen condensed cream of
   potato soup
1 soup-can milk
1 tablespoon instant minced onion
1 tablespoon chopped parsley
Dash pepper

• • •

⅓ cup shredded Parmesan cheese

Prepare potatoes according to basic recipe on package. Combine remaining ingredients except cheese. Heat till soup thaws; add to drained potatoes, mixing gently.

Turn mixture into 10x6x1½-inch baking dish. Sprinkle with cheese. Bake in moderate oven (350°) 35 minutes or till lightly browned. Top with parsley. Serves 6.

Here's a quick and easy dress-up that turns a meat loaf into an attractive company main dish

Give meat loaf a fine figure. The easy way is to shape mixture in the shallow pan that it bakes in. Sculpt sides high—you'll have a prettier loaf. For a tailored version with straight sides, press the meat lightly in oiled *loaf* pan, then *unmold* in shallow pan. For a fancy meat loaf, press mixture into lightly oiled ring mold; invert on shallow pan, remove the mold.

Score top of meat loaf for a handsome finish. The handle of a wooden spoon—or a table knife —makes this a snap. "Draw" any design you like, we show neatly spaced diagonal lines. Fill the grooves with chili sauce or catsup—tasty trim bakes right on the meat loaf.

Another tasty topper is cheese. Cut process cheese slices in shapes, or sprinkle shredded process cheese over; dash with paprika.

. . . .

It's Lamb Night!

Lamb-chop Broil *or*
Lamb Kabobs
Broiled Tomatoes   Minted Pears
Peas with Mushrooms
Carrot Curls   Radish Roses
Ice Cream-Cake Roll
Coffee

. . . .

Lamb Kabobs

Serve all-meat kabobs as part of broiler meal. Another time, make Kabobs with Mushrooms; serve with pilaf, broiled tomatoes, relishes—

  1 envelope onion-soup mix
  1 cup salad oil
  ½ cup red wine vinegar
  1 tablespoon soy sauce
  2 pounds boneless lamb, cut in
    1-inch cubes

Combine onion-soup mix, salad oil, vinegar, and soy sauce; add lamb cubes and stir to coat. Refrigerate overnight or let stand at room temperature 2 or 3 hours, turning meat occasionally. Fill skewers. Sprinkle with freshly ground pepper.

Broil 4 to 5 inches from heat 8 to 10 minutes or till done, basting now and then with marinade. Serve on pilaf, if desired. Makes 6 to 8 servings.

Kabobs with Mushrooms: On skewers, alternate marinated lamb squares from recipe above with mushroom caps and quartered green peppers. (For easier skewering, dip mushrooms and green-pepper pieces in boiling water for a minute.) Broil as above.

Broiled Tomatoes

Halve 3 tomatoes; score cut surfaces, making ½-inch squares. (Fresh dill on hand? Snip a little over tomatoes.) Mix ¾ cup soft bread crumbs and ⅓ cup shredded process American cheese; sprinkle on tomatoes.

Broil 4 inches from heat about 5 minutes. Top with snipped parsley, if you wish.

Minted Pears

Place canned pear halves, hollow side up, beside lamb chops or kabobs last 5 to 8 minutes. Fill with mint jelly toward end of broiling time. Serve with chops.

Peas with Mushrooms

  ⅓ cup chopped onion
  2 tablespoons butter or margarine
  1 1-pound can peas, drained
  1 3-ounce can (⅜ cup) broiled
    sliced mushrooms, drained
  1 teaspoon sugar
  ½ teaspoon salt
  Dash pepper
  Dash thyme

Cook onion in butter till tender but not brown; stir in remaining ingredients. Cover; heat over *low* heat. Makes 4 servings.

Ice Cream-Cake Roll

  4 egg yolks
  ¼ cup sugar
  ½ teaspoon vanilla
  4 egg whites
  ½ cup sugar
  ¾ cup sifted cake flour
  1 teaspoon baking powder
  ¼ teaspoon salt
  1 quart ice cream

Beat egg yolks till thick and lemon-colored; gradually beat in ¼ cup sugar; add vanilla.

Beat egg whites till soft peaks form. Gradually add ½ cup sugar and beat till stiff peaks form. Fold yolks into whites. Sift together flour, baking powder, and salt; fold into egg mixture.

Spread batter evenly in greased, waxed-paper-lined 15½x10½x1-inch jelly roll pan. Bake at 375° about 12 minutes or till done.

Loosen sides, turn out on towel sprinkled with sifted confectioners' sugar. Peel off paper. Trim crusts. Starting at narrow end, roll cake and towel together; cool on rack.

Unroll, remove towel. Stir 1 quart of ice cream (his favorite flavor) just to soften; gently spread on cake. Roll up. Wrap in waxed paper; freeze. Slice just before serving. Makes 10 1-inch slices.

**Lamb-chop Broil
is easy on the cook!**

Dinner's ready—broiler fast! Platter partners, juicy pear halves filled with mint jelly and bright red tomatoes, heat alongside meat. Another time, broil chicken halves, peaches.

Lamb-chop Broil—you brush on Italian dressing for zesty flavor.

Shown here are the thrifty lamb shoulder chops, cut ½ to ¾ inch thick. Some are arm chops (they have the round bones), the others are blade chops. For a real splurge, choose thick loin or rib lamb chops.

Using a sharp knife, slash the fat edge at intervals (but don't cut into the meat). This allows the lamb chops to lie flat while broiling —no cupping up.

Place chops on the broiler-pan rack. To add a subtle garlic flavor, brush the meat with your favorite Italian dressing, speedy with a salad-dressing mix or with bottled dressing.

Broil the meat 3 inches from heat, about 8 to 10 minutes on the first side. Then turn chops, and brush again. Add fruit accompaniments, halved tomatoes, if desired; broil for 4 or 5 minutes longer. (Don't overcook.)

Ranch Ribs

3 to 4 pounds loin back ribs, *or*
 spareribs sawed in two strips,
 about 3 inches wide
1 cup catsup
1 tablespoon Worcestershire sauce
2 or 3 dashes hot pepper sauce
1 cup water
¼ cup vinegar
1 tablespoon sugar
1 teaspoon salt
1 teaspoon celery seed

Season ribs with salt and pepper; place in shallow roasting pan, meaty side up. Roast in very hot oven (450°) 30 minutes. Lower temperature control to 350°; continue baking 30 minutes. Spoon off excess fat.

Combine remaining ingredients; bring to boiling and pour over ribs. Continue baking at 350° about 45 minutes or till ribs are tender, basting with sauce every 15 minutes. (If sauce gets too thick, add more water.) Makes 4 servings.

Polynesian Ribs

Make *Polynesian Sauce:* Combine ½ cup soy sauce, ½ cup catsup, 3 tablespoons brown sugar, 2 to 3 teaspoons grated gingerroot *or* 1 teaspoon ground ginger, and 1 teaspoon monosodium glutamate; let stand overnight before using.

Rub 3 pounds loin backs or meaty spareribs on both sides with ¼ cup sugar and 1 teaspoon smoked salt; let stand 2 hours. Brush with Polynesian Sauce; let stand at least an hour—preferably longer. Bake as for Ranch Ribs, brush ribs with sauce.

Potatoes with Cheese Sauce

The three "greats" with baked potatoes (sour cream, cheese, and butter) add up to a wonderful creamy, no-cook sauce—

5 or 6 baking potatoes
Sauce:
½ cup dairy sour cream
¼ cup soft butter or margarine
1 cup shredded sharp process
 American cheese
2 tablespoons chopped green onions

Scrub potatoes. For crunchy skins, bake as is; for soft skins, rub with fat. Bake alongside ribs for last 60 to 80 minutes. When spuds are done, roll gently under hand to make mealy inside. To keep mealy, immediately cut crisscross in top of each with fork tines; press ends, pushing up to fluff. Ladle Cheese Sauce generously into the potatoes.

Cheese Sauce: Combine sour cream, butter, cheese and onions, mixing well.

Barbecue Bread

½ cup (1 stick) soft butter or
 margarine
1 tablespoon prepared mustard
½ cup shredded Parmesan cheese
¼ cup snipped parsley
1 loaf French bread, about 18
 inches long

Combine first 4 ingredients. Slash bread on the bias in 1-inch slices, cutting to, *but not through*, bottom crust. Spread butter mixture generously on one side of each slice. Wrap loaf in foil. Heat in moderate oven (350°) about 25 to 30 minutes or till hot through.

Pineapple Parfaits

1 1-pound can (2 cups) fruit cocktail,
 chilled, well drained
1 6-ounce can frozen pineapple-juice
 concentrate
1 quart vanilla ice cream

Combine fruit cocktail and pineapple concentrate. Alternate layers of ice cream and fruit mixture in chilled parfait glasses. Garnish with pineapple chunks and maraschino cherries. Makes 6 servings.

Standing Rib Roast of Beef

Select a 2- or 3-rib standing rib roast of beef (4 to 5 pounds). Place fat side up in roasting pan; season with salt and pepper. Insert the meat thermometer so tip reaches center of the thickest muscle. Place pan in slow oven (325°). Do not add water; do not cover.

Roast to desired degree of doneness. Allow 20 to 22 minutes *per pound* for rare roast, 24 to 27 minutes *per pound* for medium, and 29 to 32 minutes *per pound* for well-done roast. Meat thermometer will read 140° for rare, 160° for medium, 170° for well-done beef. Count on 2 to 3 servings per pound of meat.

Rolled Rib Roast of Beef

Select boned and rolled rib roast. Prepare and roast as for standing rib roast, but allow 30 to 32 minutes *per pound* for rare, 34 to 37 minutes *per pound* for medium, 39 to 42 minutes *per pound* for well-done. Meat thermometer will read 140° for rare, 160° for medium, and 170° for well-done. Let roast stand 15 minutes to firm before carving. Allow 3 to 4 servings per pound of meat.

Roast Potatoes

Pare medium potatoes; cook in boiling salted water 15 minutes; drain. About 45 minutes before roast is done (oven temperature, 325°), place hot potatoes in drippings around the roast, turning potatoes to coat.

Roast till potatoes are done, turning occasionally to baste. Salt lightly.

Creamed Onions

18 to 20 medium onions
⅓ cup salad oil
3 tablespoons all-purpose flour
1½ cups milk
1 cup shredded process cheese
Peanuts, chopped

Peel onions and cook in boiling salted water until tender; drain. Blend salad oil and flour; stir in milk and cook slowly until thick, stirring constantly.

Add the cheese; stir until melted. Add onions and heat through. Place in serving bowl, and sprinkle with chopped peanuts. Makes 6 to 8 servings.

Citrus Fruit Bowl

Overlap a circle of grapefruit sections and orange slices. To remove pretty sections from citrus fruit, pare fruit closely, then cut between membranes and lift the segments out.

Cut avocado balls with a melon ball cutter or measuring teaspoon (or cut cubes). Arrange avocado balls atop the grapefruit and orange sections.

Pass *Honeyberry Dressing:* Beat smooth ½ cup jellied cranberry sauce. Stir in ¼ cup honey and 1 teaspoon lemon juice.

Caramel Fluff Pie

½ pound (28) vanilla caramels
1 cup milk
Dash salt
1 envelope (1 tablespoon) unflavored gelatin
¼ cup cold water
1 cup whipping cream, whipped
½ cup chopped pecans
1 teaspoon vanilla
. . .
1 9-inch Gingersnap Crust

Melt caramels in milk in top of double boiler over boiling water, stirring occasionally. (Or heat over low heat, stirring constantly.) Add salt. Soften gelatin in cold water; add to caramels; stir to dissolve. Chill till mixture is partially set. Fold in whipped cream, nuts, and vanilla. Fill crust. Chill 2 or 3 hours or till firm.

The kids are cooking!

Picnic in the Kitchen

Saucy Franks
Totem-pole Relishes
Pineapple Upside-down Cake
Cold Milk

Add potato chips, if you like.

Chicken Dinner

Oven-fried Chicken
Hot Buttered Peas
Apple Salad Cups
Choco-Almond Velvet Milk

Serve this for Sunday dinner.

Burger Special

Cheeseburger Towers
Thousand Island Dressing 'n
Lettuce
Quick Frosty Ambrosia

This meal is a quickie to fix!

Cooking is great fun! Sure, you've known that ever since you had pretend tea parties. But now you're about to fix dinner for the family. Be safe . . . cook with care. Talk it over with Cook, Sr. Watch out for "ouches." Careful with the knife. Use a potholder to keep a cool hand. Mother will tell you how to use the range. Be sure your hands are dry when you plug in or disconnect an appliance. Read through your recipe for the ingredients and the equipment you'll need. O.K. Kitchen, here we come.

Oven-fried Chicken

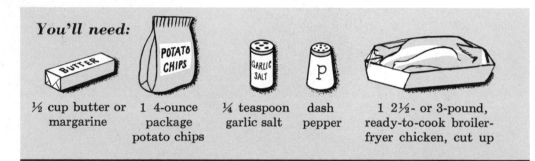

You'll need:

½ cup butter or margarine	1 4-ounce package potato chips	¼ teaspoon garlic salt	dash pepper	1 2½- or 3-pound, ready-to-cook broiler-fryer chicken, cut up

Take out: Jellyroll pan, rolling pin, waxed paper, measuring cups and spoons, skillet, potholders

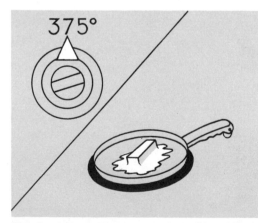

Set the oven temperature control at 375°. Melt butter in a small skillet. This recipe will make about 4 servings.

Crush potato chips with rolling pin before opening. Mix crushed potato chips with garlic salt and pepper on waxed paper.

The whole family will enjoy Oven-fried Chicken. It goes into the oven in a jacket of seasoned potato-chip crumbs. No prebrowning, no turning. Out it comes one hour later.

Dip chicken in melted butter, then roll in potato-chip crumbs. This will make the chicken crispy and good.

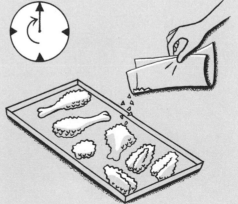

Place pieces on pan, skin side up, so they do not touch. Pour rest of butter, crumbs over chicken. Bake 1 hour (do not turn).

Saucy Franks

Count on these to make a hit with the whole family—they're terrific

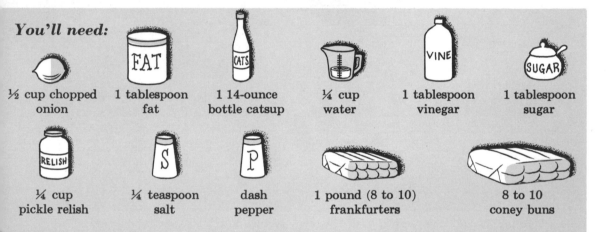

You'll need:

½ cup chopped onion	1 tablespoon fat	1 14-ounce bottle catsup	¼ cup water	1 tablespoon vinegar	1 tablespoon sugar
¼ cup pickle relish	¼ teaspoon salt	dash pepper	1 pound (8 to 10) frankfurters		8 to 10 coney buns

Take out: Skillet, measuring cups and spoons, wooden spoon, paring knife, potholder

Preheat electric skillet to 250°. (Or use ordinary skillet on medium heat.) Cook onion in hot fat till tender, but not brown.

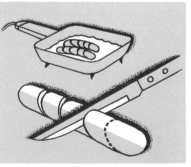

Stir in catsup, water, vinegar, sugar, relish, salt, pepper. For fancy franks, cut round, round, *very lightly!* Add to sauce in skillet; lower temperature to 220°.

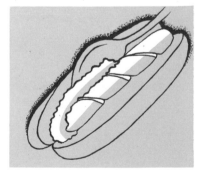

Cover; simmer till hot through, about 15 minutes. Slice and toast the coney buns; butter. Spoon frankfurters and sauce into buns. Makes 8 to 10 servings.

Almost two sandwiches in one. Good!

Cheeseburger Towers

You'll need:

2 pounds
ground beef

2 teaspoons
salt

dash
pepper

6 slices process
American cheese

6 hamburger buns
split and toasted

Take out: Griddle or skillet, turner, cooky cutter, measuring spoons, potholder

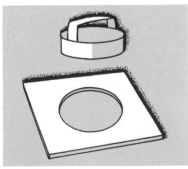

Combine meat, salt, pepper, mix lightly. Shape in 12 4-inch patties. Cook on lightly greased griddle about 3 minutes on each side. (Turn just *once*.)

Place cheese slices on wax paper. With a 2-inch cooky cutter, cut a circle from center of each cheese slice. (Slices with holes go between patties, circles atop.)

Place a patty in each bun. Add cheese slice; fill hole with catsup, mustard, pickle relish. Add second patty, cheese circle, bun.

Thousand Island Dressing

This dressing makes a lettuce wedge special!

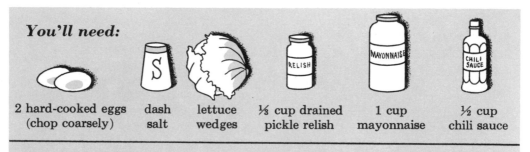

You'll need:

| 2 hard-cooked eggs (chop coarsely) | dash salt | lettuce wedges | ⅓ cup drained pickle relish | 1 cup mayonnaise | ½ cup chili sauce |

Take out: Bowl, measuring cups, paring knife, spoon

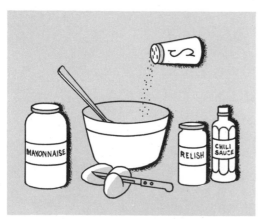

In a bowl, mix together mayonnaise, chili sauce, pickle relish, and salt. Add chopped eggs. Chill dressing in the refrigerator.

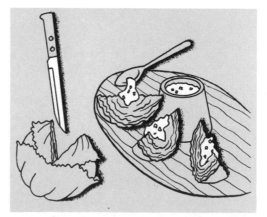

Cut a head of lettuce into wedges. Spoon dressing on the crisp lettuce wedges. Top each with pimiento strips, if you wish.

Apple Salad Cups

Cranberry juice lends a jewel look and tart flavor to these salads.

You'll need:

½ cup chopped celery

¼ teaspoon salt

¼ cup broken walnuts

1 cup chopped unpared apple

1 package lemon-flavored gelatin

1 pint bottle cranberry-juice cocktail

Take out: Measuring cups and spoons, saucepan, paring knife, spoon, bowl, potholder, six 5-ounce custard cups or small molds

Pour gelatin into bowl. Heat 1 cup of cranberry-juice cocktail; add. Stir to dissolve gelatin. Add salt and rest of cranberry-juice cocktail (cold). Chill.

When gelatin is thick and syrupy, stir in the chopped apple, celery, and nuts. Spoon the mixture into 5-ounce custard cups or small molds. Chill until firm.

To unmold, loosen around edge with small spatula. Place each atop a pineapple ring on lettuce leaf. Spoon on mayonnaise.

Totem-pole Relishes

Any combination goes! Poke skewers into plastic foam covered with crushed ice.

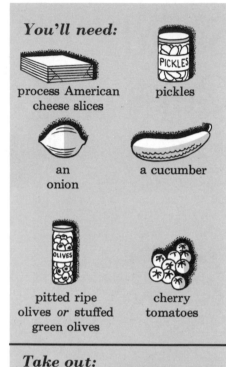

You'll need:

process American cheese slices

pickles

an onion

a cucumber

pitted ripe olives *or* stuffed green olives

cherry tomatoes

Take out:

Paring knife, cutting board, skewers

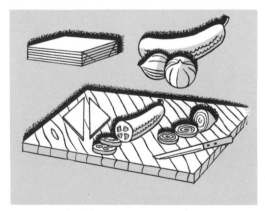

Cut the cheese slices corner to corner to make triangles. Then cut the onion and cucumber in generous slices.

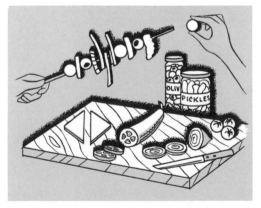

Peg the relishes on skewers. Make each totem-pole include some of everything! Stand up in a bowl of crushed ice.

Quick Frosty Ambrosia

You'll need:

1 14-ounce can frozen pineapple chunks

½ cup moist shredded or flaked coconut

1 banana, sliced

1 pint fresh strawberries

Take out:

Can opener
paring knife
bowl
4 dessert dishes
spoon

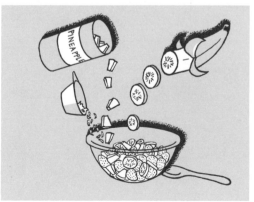

It's a cool and refreshing dessert, just right to top off any meal! Pretty trim—whole berries.

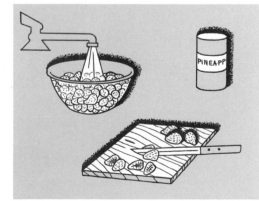

Let can of pineapple chunks stand at room temperature about 1 hour. Wash berries, take off stems. Cut berries in two.

Toss strawberries with banana, pineapple, and coconut. Spoon into 4 dessert dishes. Serve while pineapple is still frosty.

Super smooth and delicious! It's like a frozen milkshake, only better!

Choco-Almond Velvet

You'll need: ⅔ cup canned chocolate syrup, ⅔ cup sweetened condensed milk, 2 cups whipping cream, ½ teaspoon vanilla, ⅓ cup chopped toasted almonds. (Or buy slivered blanched almonds. Bake in shallow pan at 350° (stir often) till pale brown.)

Take out: Can opener, bowl, measuring cups and spoons, egg beater, spoon, refrigerator tray, dessert dishes

In mixing bowl, combine chocolate syrup, condensed milk, cream, and vanilla. Chill till very cold. Whip till mixture forms soft peaks and is fluffy. Fold in nuts.

Pile into refrigerator tray and freeze until firm. Spoon into dessert dishes. If you wish, sprinkle with more toasted almonds and serve. Makes 8 to 10 servings.

Pineapple Upside-down Cake

Bottoms up, it's "frosted"!

You'll need: 2 tablespoons butter, ½ cup brown sugar, 4 canned pineapple slices, 7 maraschino cherries, 1 loaf-size yellow cake mix.

Take out: Measuring cups and spoons, round ovenware cake dish, bowl, can opener, cake rack, potholders.

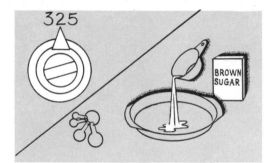

Set temperature control at 325°. Melt butter; pour into 8¼ x1¾-inch round ovenware cake dish. (Or a 9x1½-inch round metal cake pan.) Blend in sugar; pat out evenly.

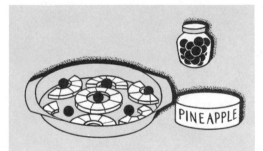

Place 1 canned pineapple slice in the center; arrange 3 halved pineapple slices and the maraschino cherries around the whole slice to make a design. This is the "frosting."

Prepare batter from cake mix following package directions, *using pineapple juice instead of liquid called for* (add water if not enough). Pour batter over fruit.

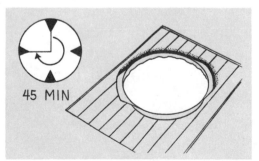

Bake 45 minutes (if using metal pan bake 35 minutes at 350°). Cool in pan on rack 10 minutes. Turn upside down on serving plate. Cut and serve warm.

Buy a bargain... fix a feast!

Plan on variation from cuts like short ribs and brisket.
Make hash from yesterday's roast, custard from extra egg yolks.

"Choice" eating that is easy on the bank

Our Braised Short Ribs are tender, flavorful, *and* offer a wonderful bonus—onion gravy that hints of sauerbraten flavor—to spoon over the meat, and mashed potatoes. This is man-style eating! Serve with buttered broccoli or corn and a tossed green salad. And top off the meal with cooling Cranberry Sherbet. The meatman can cut short ribs from chuck, ribs, or short plate.

Eat well on little money!

Braised Short Ribs with Onion Gravy

Trim excess fat from 3 pounds beef short ribs; heat fat in Dutch oven. Roll short ribs in flour; *slowly* brown on all sides in the hot fat. When thoroughly browned, spoon off fat. Sprinkle meat with 1 teaspoon salt and dash pepper; add 1 medium onion, sliced, and ½ cup water.

Cover and simmer* (do not boil) till tender, 2 to 2½ hours. (Add more water if needed during cooking.) Lift meat from the stock to a warm platter; keep meat hot while you make Onion Gravy. Serves 6.

*Or cover and cook in slow to moderate oven (325° to 350°) 2 to 2½ hours.

Onion Gravy: Skim fat from meat stock; reserve 2 tablespoons. Measure stock, add hot water to make 2 cups; set aside.

Brown ¼ cup sugar in the 2 tablespoons fat. Add 4 medium onions, sliced; cook and stir till tender; push aside. Add 2 tablespoons flour; brown slightly. Remove pan from heat.

Slowly stir in meat stock, 2 tablespoons vinegar and ½ teaspoon kitchen bouquet. Return to heat and cook, stirring constantly, till gravy is bubbling all over. Season to taste with salt and pepper.

Continue *cooking slowly* about 5 minutes, stirring now and then. Serve hot with short ribs or over fluffy mashed potatoes.

Cranberry Sherbet

Let this be the refreshing finale to your big meal. It's pretty pink and ever so smooth. Terrific as a cool appetizer, too—

¾ cup sugar
½ envelope (1½ teaspoons)
  unflavored gelatin
Dash salt
1 pint bottle (2 cups) cranberry-
  juice cocktail
      • • •
2 tablespoons lemon juice

In saucepan, mix sugar, gelatin, and salt. Stir in 1 *cup* of the cranberry-juice cocktail. Heat and stir over medium heat till sugar and gelatin dissolve. Remove from heat; add remaining cranberry-juice cocktail and the lemon juice.

Freeze in refrigerator tray till firm; break in chunks and beat with an electric beater till smooth.* Return to refrigerator tray; freeze for several hours. Serve in sherbets. Trim with mint sprigs. Serves 8.

*Or freeze till partially frozen; beat smooth with a rotary beater.

Flavorful and economical, too →

This savory meal is simple to prepare. It's Beef Brisket with Vegetables—meat, potatoes, and onions bake lazily together till meat is temptingly brown and fork-tender and vegetables are done. Recipe is on page 38.

Beef Brisket with Vegetables

Trim excess fat from 3 pounds fresh boneless beef brisket. Place meat in Dutch oven with *tight-fitting* lid. Sprinkle with 1½ teaspoons salt and dash *each* of pepper and paprika. Add 1 bay leaf. Cut 3 medium onions in thick slices and arrange over meat. (Do not add water.) Cover and bake in slow oven (300° to 325°) 3½ to 4½ hours or till very tender.

Last hour of baking arrange 6 medium potatoes, pared and halved lengthwise, around brisket; sprinkle potatoes with ½ teaspoon salt and dash pepper; cover and continue to bake till done, turning and basting potatoes every 15 minutes. (If meat and potatoes need more browning uncover the last 30 minutes—remember to turn and baste potatoes.) Skim off excess fat. Serve brisket with the good meat juices or thicken gravy. To carve, cut across the grain, slanting knife slightly and making *thin* slices. Pass bowl of prepared horse-radish. Makes 9 servings.

Cherry Puff

It shares the oven with Beef Brisket—

1 No. 2 can (2½ cups) pitted tart
   red cherries, drained
½ cup liquid from cherries
½ cup sugar
2 tablespoons quick-cooking
   tapioca

• • •

2 egg whites
Dash salt
¼ teaspoon cream of tartar
2 egg yolks
⅓ cup sugar
⅓ cup sifted cake flour

Chop cherries; add cherry liquid, sugar, and tapioca. Simmer mixture 5 minutes, stirring constantly.

Beat egg whites until foamy; add salt and cream of tartar; beat stiff. Beat egg yolks until thick and lemon-colored; add sugar gradually; beat thoroughly. Fold egg yolks into whites. Sift flour over, fold in.

Pour cherry mixture into 8x8x2-inch baking dish. Pour batter on top. Bake in slow oven (325°) 30 to 35 minutes. Cut in squares. Serve with ice cream. Serves 6.

Ham-bone Bean Soup

1 pound (2⅛ cups) dry navy beans
1 1½-pound meaty ham bone, *or*
   1½ pounds smoked hocks
½ teaspoon salt
6 whole black peppers
1 bay leaf
1 medium onion, sliced

Thoroughly wash beans. Cover with 2 quarts cold water; bring to boiling; boil gently 2 minutes. Remove from heat; cover and let stand 1 hour. (Do not drain.)

Add ham bone, seasonings. Cover; heat to boiling; boil gently till beans are tender, about 3 to 3½ hours. Add onion last half hour. Remove ham bone; if desired, mash beans slightly with potato masher. Cut ham off bone; return meat to soup. Season to taste with salt and pepper. Serves 6.

Tapioca Fluff

Combine 1 quart milk, ¼ cup quick-cooking tapioca, ½ cup sugar, and ¼ tea-spoon salt. Let stand 5 minutes. Add 3 slightly beaten egg yolks. Bring quickly to boiling; stir constantly. Remove from heat (mixture will be thin); add 1½ teaspoons vanilla.

Beat 3 egg whites till stiff. Put about ⅓ of the beaten egg whites in large bowl; slowly stir in the hot mixture. Fold in re-maining egg white, leaving little "pillows" of egg white. Chill. Serve in sherbets. Top with currant jelly. Serves 8 to 10.

Hearty soup for the family →

Smoked hocks or a meaty ham bone imparts the rich flavor. Dish up the soup while it's still too hot to sample. Go-with: corn sticks.

How to save money at the food store

Food bills don't pinch just now and then —they bite off about 20 per cent of your daily budget, according to Uncle Sam's figures. And there's no way out of it—you have to eat regularly! But you don't have to eat the same old thing, in the same old way, week after week, in order to balance the budget and the diet. There are many good ways to feed a family well—and do it on less money than you're spending now!

Plan meals in advance

Be smart—list exact needs and spending limit before every trip to the grocery store —and stick to them. That means you've got to plan meals ahead. (It's worth it!)

Go in for specials

Quality of the meat sold should be a big factor in where you shop. The biggest part of the food dollar goes for meat, and it can be the biggest food saving.

Stock up on weekend specials, but be sure it is something you really need. One of the best ways to make the home freezer pay for itself is to buy enough on special to last awhile. But don't buy too much.

Buy big sometimes

Buy in quantity only if you have storage space. Careful on perishables. You may find good buys in apples or potatoes by the bushel, but if your house has no cool basement, these can spoil faster than you can eat them. You aren't saving money when you toss half the bushel away.

Buy top grade some of the time

High price doesn't guarantee high quality. A 49-cent pound of ground beef packs more nutrition than a $1.29-pound of T-bone, because it contains no waste.

Sometimes it is extravagant to buy top quality. If beans are to be buttered, you want the best. If you plan a casserole with bacon and onions, a lesser grade is fine.

Be flexible in your food plan

If the lettuce on your list costs twice as much this week as last, substitute cabbage. Unseasonal heavy freezes can wipe out a fruit or vegetable crop. If the affected area supplies most of the nation's needs, you can count on a higher price.

Yes, use convenience foods!

Mass production has worked a modern miracle in providing many convenience foods at bargain prices. Know when you can save and when you can't by "starting from scratch."

Most families use a combination of foods —and this is as it should be. Home cooking is creative and delicious, but you can get homemade flavor by adding your own personal touch to convenience foods, too.

Save more by cooking more

When beef pot roast is on special, get it. Serve part as pot roast (turn leftovers into meat pie or hash), part as mock Stroganoff (use meat tenderizer first!).

A whole ham can be sliced by the butcher into frying slices, a baking slice, and two roasts, the butt and the shank, (or use shank roast for bean soup!).

Serve company "next best"

Use candlelight to make guest fare of a great casserole. Use inexpensive substitutes for party dress-ups—like pate. Mash liver sausage, thin with sour cream; season.

Leftovers...
good to the last bite!

Chicken-'n-Stuffing Scallop

Prepare ½ 8-ounce package (1¾ cups) herb-seasoned stuffing according to package directions for dry stuffing. Spread in a 10x6x1½-inch baking dish. Top with 1½ cups cubed cooked chicken.

In saucepan, melt ¼ cup butter; blend in ¼ cup all-purpose flour, and dash in salt and pepper. Add 2 cups cooled chicken broth; cook and stir till mixture thickens. Stir small amount of hot mixture into 3 slightly beaten eggs; return to hot mixture; pour over chicken.

Bake in slow oven (325°) 35 to 40 minutes or till knife inserted off-center comes out clean. Let stand 5 minutes to set; cut in squares and serve hot with Pimiento Mushroom Sauce. Makes 6 servings.

Pimiento Mushroom Sauce

Mix ½ can condensed cream of mushroom soup, 2 tablespoons milk, ½ cup dairy sour cream, and 2 tablespoons chopped pimiento. Heat and stir constantly till hot through. Makes 6 servings. Serve with Chicken-'n-Stuffing Scallop.

Chicken-salad Special

1½ cups coarsely diced cooked chicken
1 cup diced celery
¼ cup mayonnaise
2 tablespoons chopped sweet pickle
1½ tablespoons lemon juice

Lightly toss together all ingredients. Season to taste with salt and pepper. Chill. Serve atop crisp lettuce. Serves 3.

Chicken-'n-Stuffing Scallop It's stuffing and chicken baked in a custard. The family will want you to *plan* for this one! Or double, bake in 13x9x2-inch dish and serve the club.

Best Oven Hash

A perfect encore for leftover roast beef and potatoes. It's expertly seasoned with Worcestershire sauce and onion, has evaporated milk for richness. Crown hash in traditional fashion with poached eggs.

Best Oven Hash

This is real meat and potatoes fare. No hint of "leftover" here! Tastes like a ""first run"—

1½ cups coarsely ground cooked beef
1 cup coarsely ground cooked
   potatoes
½ cup coarsely ground onion
¼ cup chopped parsley
1 teaspoon salt
Dash pepper
2 teaspoons Worcestershire sauce
1 6-ounce can (⅔ cup) evaporated
   milk

• • •

⅓ cup slightly crushed corn flakes
1 tablespoon butter or margarine,
   melted

Lightly mix beef, potatoes, onion, parsley, salt, pepper, Worcestershire sauce, and milk. Turn into greased 1-quart casserole. Mix corn flakes and butter; sprinkle over top. Bake in moderate oven (350°) 30 minutes or till heated through. Pass catsup and mustard. Makes 4 servings.

Skillet Ham Salad

Put leftover ham and potatoes to good use. Hot and hearty, the kind men enjoy—

¼ cup chopped green onions
¼ cup chopped green pepper
2 cups diced cooked ham
1 tablespoon fat

• • •

3 or 4 medium potatoes, cooked,
   diced (3 cups)
¼ teaspoon salt
Dash pepper
¼ cup mayonnaise or salad
   dressing

• • •

½ pound sharp process American
   cheese, diced (1½ cups)

Cook onions, green pepper, and meat in hot fat, stirring occasionally, till meat is lightly browned. Add potatoes, salt, pepper, and mayonnaise. Heat, mixing lightly. Stir in cheese; heat just till it begins to melt. Garnish with green onions, if desired. Makes 4 servings.

Sandwiches Stroganoff

Canned gravy with sour cream—grand finale for Sunday's roast—

Cook 1 tablespoon chopped onion in 1 tablespoon butter or margarine till tender but not brown; stir in 1 can (1¼ cups) beef gravy, ¼ cup dairy sour cream, 1 tablespoon cooking sherry, ¼ teaspoon monosodium glutamate, and dash basil.

Add 6 slices leftover roast beef; heat 8 to 10 minutes, stirring occasionally. Serve over hot toast. Makes 6 servings.

Barbecued Pork Sandwiches

Cook ¼ cup chopped onion in 1 tablespoon hot oil till tender but not brown. Stir in one 8-ounce can (1 cup) seasoned tomato sauce, ¼ to ⅓ cup bottled steak sauce, 2 tablespoons brown sugar, and dash salt; bring to boiling. Add 1½ to 2 cups thinly sliced roast pork. Reduce heat, cover, and cook gently about 10 minutes. Serve over hot toast or in toasted hamburger buns. Makes 6 to 8 servings.

Winter Garden Loaf

2 3-ounce packages lemon-
   flavored gelatin
3½ cups hot water
3 tablespoons vinegar
½ teaspoon salt
9 to 12 canned whole green beans
3 or 4 long strips pimiento

• • •

1 cup cooked cauliflowerets
½ cup cooked sliced carrots
¼ cup diced celery
¼ cup sliced radishes
¼ cup sliced green onions

Dissolve gelatin in hot water; add vinegar and salt. Pour about ½ inch of gelatin mixture into 8½x4½x2½-inch loaf pan. Chill till set. Divide beans in 3 or 4 bundles; circle each with pimiento strip. Arrange on gelatin in pan. Chill remaining gelatin till partially set; pour enough over beans to cover; chill until firm.

Meanwhile combine remaining gelatin with rest of vegetables (but do not chill). Pour over firm gelatin in pan, then chill till set. Unmold on lettuce. Serves 8.

Winter Garden Loaf   Cooked green beans, carrots, cauliflower, or other vegetables make an attractive comeback in lemon-flavored gelatin. Loaf tastes just like spring—radishes and celery add crispness.

Caramel Custard is like velvet. And it's good for you—with half a dozen egg yolks! Caramelized sugar is the delicious sauce. Invert custards, sauce runs down.

Perfect Bread Pudding is a classic way to use the last of the loaf. Brown sugar, cinnamon, and plenty of plump raisins are the key to its old-time flavor.

Burgers and Potatoes

Form one pound hamburger into four patties; broil 3 to 4 inches from heat about 6 minutes; turn, broil 2 minutes. Place Cheese Potatoes beside patties; broil till patties are done and potatoes are hot through, about 4 minutes. Serves 4.

Cheese Potatoes: Peel two leftover whole cooked potatoes; slice ¼ inch thick. Coat with 2 tablespoons melted butter. Sprinkle tops with ½ cup shredded sharp process cheese. Broil as directed above.

Caramel Custard

Combine 6 to 7 slightly beaten egg yolks, ¼ cup sugar, and ¼ teaspoon salt; slowly stir in 2 cups scalded milk, slightly cooled; add ½ teaspoon vanilla. Set aside.

Melt ½ cup sugar in heavy skillet over low heat, *stirring all the time.* As soon as syrup turns a pretty golden brown, remove from heat. Spoon 1 tablespoon syrup into each of six 5-ounce custard cups using spoon to quickly swirl syrup so bottom and sides of cup are coated.

Set cups in shallow pan on oven rack. Pour hot water around 1 inch deep. Pour custard into cups. Dash with nutmeg.

Bake at 325° for 40 to 45 minutes, or till knife inserted off-center comes out clean.

Perfect Bread Pudding

Combine 2¼ cups milk and 2 slightly beaten eggs; pour over 2 cups 1-inch day-old bread cubes. Add ½ cup brown sugar, 1 teaspoon cinnamon, 1 teaspoon vanilla, ¼ teaspoon salt, and ½ cup light or dark seedless raisins; toss lightly to blend.

Spread mixture in greased 8x8x2-inch baking dish. Set dish in shallow pan on oven rack. Pour hot water around it 1 inch deep. Bake in moderate oven (350°) about 35 to 40 minutes or till knife inserted half-way between center and outside edge comes out clean. Makes 9 servings.

Heavenly Hawaiian Sherbet

Soften ½ envelope (½ tablespoon) un-flavored gelatin in 2 tablespoons cold water; dissolve over hot water. Combine 2 cups buttermilk, ¾ cup sugar, one 9-ounce can (1 cup) crushed pineapple, 1 teaspoon vanilla, gelatin; mix well. Freeze in refrigerator tray till firm.

Break in chunks; turn into chilled bowl; beat smooth with electric or rotary beater. Beat 1 egg white till soft peaks form; gradually add ¼ cup sugar and beat till stiff peaks form. Fold into pineapple mixture. Return quickly to *cold* tray. Freeze until firm. Makes 4 to 6 servings.

Butter Sponge Cake

You can use those extra egg yolks here—

1 cup sifted cake flour
1 teaspoon baking powder
¼ cup butter, melted
½ teaspoon vanilla
½ cup milk, scalded
6 egg yolks
1 cup sugar
1 recipe Orange Butter Frosting

Sift together flour and baking powder. Add butter and vanilla to scalded milk and keep hot. Beat egg yolks till thick and lemon-colored; gradually beat in sugar. Quickly add flour mixture; stir just till mixed. Gently stir in the hot milk mixture.

Pour into greased 9x9x2-inch pan; bake in moderate oven (350°) 30 to 35 minutes or till done. Cool thoroughly and frost with Orange Butter Frosting. Cut in squares, center each with walnut half.

Orange Butter Frosting

Thoroughly cream ¼ cup butter and 2 cups sifted confectioners' sugar; add 2 teaspoons grated orange peel. Stir in 1 tablespoon orange juice or enough to make of spreading consistency; beat smooth. Spread on cooled Butter Sponge Cake.

Coconut Torte Dessert

Combine 1 cup graham-cracker crumbs, ½ cup flaked coconut, and ½ cup chopped walnuts. Beat 4 egg whites, 1 teaspoon vanilla, and ¼ teaspoon salt till soft peaks form; gradually add 1 cup sugar, beating till very stiff peaks form and all sugar has dissolved. Fold graham-cracker mixture into egg-white mixture. Spread in well-greased 9-inch pie plate. Bake at 350° about 30 minutes. Cool. Cut in wedges and top with scoops of butter-brickle ice cream (takes 1 pint). Makes 6 to 8 servings.

Butter Sponge Cake   Truly delectable eating! It's an airy, tender cake the color of sunshine. Top with Orange Butter Frosting and crown each piece with a walnut half. Just right to serve with afternoon tea.

Snow-capped Apricot Chiffon Pie

Oriental—good!

Low-calorie cooking

Here are recipes to cheer your dieter—main dishes, salads, and desserts that look and taste every bit as good as their high-calorie cousins. Plus— tips to tell the calorie-counter how to eat out and enjoy it!

Low in calories... and high in goodness

Cut calories, but enjoy it. Give yourself plenty of encouragement when dieting.
- Weigh first thing in the morning.
- Count the calories you don't eat. This will keep your spirits high.

And "stretch" the calories of your reducing meals into a lot of eating satisfaction.
- Don't skip meals.
- Do skip the "in-betweens." Save a serving (like gelatin salad) for your snack.
- Slice foods thinly, and spread them in such a way on your plate that a little tends to look like a lot.
- Take your time in eating.
- Stop before you're full.

You *can* eat out while dieting. Here are foods to order that disguise the fact you're dieting, and still give you a dandy reducer's meal.

Appetizer: Consomme or any clear soup (not creamed), melon, fresh-fruit cup, grapefruit, tomato juice. Choose one.

Main course: Lean meat or fish. Cut away visible fat, if any. Choose two vegetables, preferably one green and one yellow.

Salad: Lettuce, endive, Bibb lettuce, escarole, water cress, cabbage, tomatoes, aspic. A chef's salad makes a good main-course lunch. Use tomato juice for dressing.

Bread: Bread and rolls are fine foods, and reasonable amounts are allowed in all except very-low-calorie reducing diets. Just remember your quota: Pass up sweet rolls, sugar-coated cinnamon buns.

Dessert: Raw, canned or stewed fruits (you needn't eat all the syrupy juices), berries, melon, baked custard.

Beverage: Coffee or tea without cream or sugar, milk or buttermilk.

If you are invited to a dinner party, you can "save" some item allowed you in a previous meal in the day. Consume this food in the big meal later.

Beef Oriental

2 tablespoons salad oil
1 pound sirloin tips, sliced in strips, ¼ inch thick (across grain)

• • •

⅓ cup soy sauce
⅓ cup water
1 tablespoon sugar
1 teaspoon monosodium glutamate
2 cups 1-inch bias-cut celery slices*
2 cups 1-inch bias-cut green onions*
1 green pepper, cut in ¼-inch strips

• • •

2 5-ounce cans (about 1¼ cups) water chestnuts, drained and sliced
1 6-ounce can (1⅓ cups) broiled sliced mushrooms, drained

Heat a 12-inch skillet; add salad oil. Add beef and cook briskly, turning strips over and over, 1 or 2 minutes, or just till browned. Pour soy sauce and water over; stir in sugar and monosodium glutamate.

Bring to boiling; add celery, onions, green pepper; cook and stir over high heat about 3 minutes or till vegetables are crisp-cooked. Add water chestnuts and mushrooms; cook 2 more minutes or till hot.

(If desired, thicken with 1 tablespoon cornstarch blended with 2 tablespoons cold water.) Serve with Melba toast. Makes 6 servings. *Calories per serving: 295.*

*In slicing, make long slanting cuts (almost as for Frenching green beans). Keep pieces thin—only ¼ inch thick.

Gourmet Dressing

A wonderful all-purpose dressing!—

Pour 3 tablespoons vinegar into cruet; add 1 envelope French salad-dressing mix and shake well. Add 2 tablespoons salad oil and ⅔ cup tomato juice. Shake. Serve over fruit salad or greens. Makes 1 cup. *Calories per tablespoon: 20.*

Think-thin Salad

1 1-pound can (2 cups) unsweetened
   grapefruit sections
2 envelopes lemon-flavored
   low-calorie gelatin

• • •

¾ cup dry cottage cheese
¼ cup finely chopped celery
3 maraschino cherries, cut in fourths

Drain grapefruit and add enough water to
the juice to make 2 cups. Heat *half* the
juice mixture to boiling; add to gelatin and
stir till gelatin dissolves. Add remaining
juice mixture; cool. Reserve best grapefruit
segments (about half) for top layer. Arrange remaining segments in an 8½x4½x
2½-inch loaf pan.

Carefully pour *half* of the gelatin mixture over grapefruit in pan; chill till almost
firm. Stir cottage cheese; if needed, add 1
to 2 tablespoons skim milk to make of
spreading consistency. Add celery to cottage cheese and spread over gelatin layer
to make "filling" for salad.

Meanwhile, chill remaining gelatin mixture till partially set. Arrange reserved
grapefruit and the cherry bits on top of
cheese, so each serving has built-in trim.

Carefully pour remaining gelatin mixture over top. Chill till firm (at least 4 to 5
hours or overnight). Cut in squares and
serve on leaf lettuce. Makes 6 servings.
Calories per serving: 70.

Pineapple-Cucumber Salad

1 envelope (1 tablespoon)
   unflavored gelatin
¾ cup cold water
2 8½-ounce cans (2 cups) dietetic-
   pack pineapple tidbits
¼ cup lemon juice
1 tablespoon noncaloric liquid
   sweetener
1 cup finely chopped cucumber

Soften gelatin in cold water. Drain pineapple, reserving juice. Heat pineapple juice
to boiling; add softened gelatin and stir
until dissolved. Add lemon juice and noncaloric sweetener. Chill till partially set;
fold in pineapple and cucumber.

Turn into 1-quart mold; chill till firm.
Makes 6 servings. *Calories per serving: 60.*

Tomato Aspic Mold

2 envelopes (2 tablespoons)
   unflavored gelatin
1 cup cold tomato juice
3 cups hot tomato juice
1 tablespoon grated onion and juice
2 tablespoons lemon juice
½ teaspoon salt
½ teaspoon Worcestershire sauce
Dash pepper

Soften gelatin in cold tomato juice. Dissolve in *hot* tomato juice. Add remaining
ingredients. Pour into a 5-cup ring mold.
Chill till firm. Unmold. Trim with greens.
Makes 8 servings. *Calories per serving: 35.*

Dairy Bar Dressing

2 teaspoons minced parsley
¼ cup dry, small-curd cottage cheese
1 teaspoon catsup
½ cup buttermilk or yogurt
Dash *each* salt, paprika and marjoram

Combine parsley, cottage cheese, and catsup. Stir in buttermilk. Add seasonings to
taste. Cover, keep refrigerated until serving time. Stir just before serving. Makes ⅔
cup. *Calories per tablespoon: 10.*

Tomato Soup Dressing

¼ cup salad oil
½ cup vinegar
½ can (⅔ cup) condensed tomato soup
1 teaspoon noncaloric liquid sweetener
1 tablespoon finely chopped onion
¼ teaspoon garlic salt

Combine all ingredients and blend well
with electric or rotary beater. Store covered in refrigerator. Shake before serving.
Makes 1½ cups. *Calories per tablespoon: 14.*

Cottage-cheese Delight

Blend together one 12-ounce carton (1½
cups) cream-style cottage cheese, 2 tablespoons milk and ½ teaspoon salt in electric
blender till light and fluffy. (Or beat 5
minutes with electric beater.) Makes 1⅔
cups. *Calories per tablespoon: 15.*

Heavenly Fruit Fluff

1 ½ cups pitted, halved fresh Bing
    cherries
Noncaloric sweetener to equal
    2 tablespoons sugar*

• • •

2 8½-ounce cans (2 cups) dietetic-
    pack pineapple tidbits, drained
1 2-ounce package dessert-topping
    mix

• • •

Few drops red food coloring

Sprinkle cherries with noncaloric sweetener; chill 1 hour. Add drained pineapple.
Prepare dessert-topping mix according to
package directions; add food coloring to
tint pale pink. Fold fruit into dessert-
topping mixture. Chill several hours.

Stir at serving time (if a bit too thick,
add about 1 tablespoon milk, blending
well). Spoon into sherbet dishes. Trim each
serving with sprig of fresh mint. Makes 8
servings. *Calories per serving: 100.*

*Follow label directions for amount of
noncaloric sweetener.

Apricot Chiffon Pie

Thoroughly mix 1 envelope (1 tablespoon) unflavored gelatin, ⅓ cup sugar,
and dash salt. Heat one 12-ounce can (1½
cups) apricot nectar just to boiling; add to
gelatin mixture, stirring till dissolved.

Add 1 teaspoon lemon juice and ⅛ teaspoon almond extract. Chill till partially
set. Add 2 unbeaten egg whites and beat
till soft peaks form. Pile into cooled Lacy
Coconut Crust. Chill until firm. *Calories
per serving (1/7 of pie): 180.*

Lacy Coconut Crust: Butter a 9-inch pie
plate, using 1 teaspoon butter or margarine.
Empty a 3½-ounce can (1¼ cups) flaked
coconut into pie plate; press against bottom and sides. Bake in slow oven (325°)
about 10 minutes or till edges are golden
brown. Cool. Fill as directed above.

Good enough to be "fattening"

Heavenly Fruit Fluff stands high in sherbet
dishes, but low in calories. You'll serve it
often, it's delicious. Add a fresh mint sprig
to accent the delicate pink color.

Conscience Cake

1½ envelopes (1½ tablespoons)
   unflavored gelatin
1½ cups cold water
2 slightly beaten eggs
1½ teaspoons noncaloric liquid
   sweetener
1 teaspoon grated lime peel
¼ cup lime juice
½ cup nonfat dry milk
½ cup ice water
¼ cup sugar
Few drops green food coloring

• • •

15 small or single ladyfingers, or
   strips of sponge cake cut in
   ladyfinger size
2 oranges, sectioned

Soften gelatin in cold water. Stir in eggs. Cook and stir over low heat until gelatin dissolves. Remove from heat. Add the sweetener, lime peel, and juice; chill till partially set. Mix nonfat dry milk with ice water; whip till soft peaks form. Gradually add sugar, beating to stiff peaks. Fold into gelatin mixture. Tint pale green with food coloring. Line an 8½x4½x2½-inch loaf dish with ladyfingers, allowing a little space between them; pile in lime mixture. Chill till firm (several hours or overnight). Unmold; garnish with orange sections. Makes 8 servings. *Calories per serving* (includes 2 orange sections): *125.*

Baked Vanilla Creme

2 cups reliquefied dry milk* or
   skim milk, scalded
1 teaspoon vanilla
1 tablespoon noncaloric liquid
   sweetener
6 egg yolks

To scalded milk, add the vanilla and noncaloric sweetener. Beat egg yolks until thick and lemon-colored. Stir in milk. Set five 6-ounce custard cups in shallow pan on oven rack and fill them with custard. Pour hot water around cups, 1 inch deep. Bake in slow oven (325°) about 45 minutes, or till knife inserted off-center comes out clean. Serve chilled. Makes 5 servings. *Calories per serving: 110.*
   *Follow package directions.

Surprise Cheesecake

2 envelopes (2 tablespoons)
   unflavored gelatin
½ cup sugar
¼ teaspoon salt
2 egg yolks
1 cup reliquefied nonfat dry milk*
   or skim milk
1 teaspoon grated lemon peel
3 cups cream-style cottage
   cheese, sieved
1 tablespoon lemon juice
1 teaspoon vanilla
2 egg whites
¼ cup sugar
½ cup nonfat dry milk
½ cup ice water
⅓ cup fine graham-cracker crumbs
Dash *each* cinnamon and nutmeg

Thoroughly mix gelatin, ½ cup sugar, and salt. Beat together egg yolks and milk; add to gelatin mixture and cook and stir over low heat, till gelatin is dissolved. Remove from heat; add lemon peel; cool.
   Stir in cottage cheese, lemon juice, and vanilla. Chill, stirring occasionally, until mixture mounds when spooned. Beat egg whites till soft peaks form; gradually add ¼ cup sugar and beat to stiff peaks. Combine dry milk and ice water; whip until stiff peaks form. Fold egg whites and whipped milk into gelatin mixture.
   Combine graham-cracker crumbs and spices. Sprinkle half of crumb mixture over bottom of an 8-inch spring-form pan. Pour in cheese-cake mixture. Sprinkle top with remaining crumbs. Chill till firm. Makes 12 servings. *Calories per serving: 160.*
   *Follow package directions.

Cranberry Gelatin Dessert

1 envelope (1 tablespoon)
   unflavored gelatin
¼ cup cold water
1 pint bottle (2 cups) cranberry-juice
   cocktail, heated
1 teaspoon noncaloric liquid
   sweetener

Soften gelatin in cold water. Dissolve in hot juice. Add sweetener. Pour into 5 individual molds. Chill till set.
Calories per serving: 65.

Do-ahead dinners

Call on your refrigerator and
freezer to help you put
meals on the table with little
or no effort. Most of the
work is done ahead of time.

- Main dishes on file

- Super salads

- Day-before desserts

Serve a favorite from south of the border

You get real Mexican flavor in this casserole. Tamale Pie boasts a puffy
corn-meal topper, a spicy filling of ground beef, whole kernel corn and
ripe olives. Prepare it in your "spare time" and store in the freezer
against a busy day. To go along: hot corn chips, a spinach-onion ring
salad, pickled peppers, and caramel pudding.

Keep main dishes on file

Spare minutes now, but a busy day ahead? Whip up tomorrow's main dish and park it in the refrigerator till baking time. Try our "day before" recipes—or chill your favorite casserole overnight, then allow about 30 minutes extra time in the oven.

Keep meats and main dishes on call in your freezer, too—ready to "heat and eat" at a minute's notice. They're convenient— and penny-wise. When you spy a meat bargain, buy double, cook all, freeze half!

Freezing cooked main dishes—

- Don't oversalt or overseason cooked foods—it's better to add more later.
- Don't overcook foods to be frozen.
- Cool quickly before packaging; freeze immediately in meal-size portions.
- Don't refreeze cooked foods.
- Use frozen foods within the recommended storage time (see chart).

Meat dishes: If roasts are whole, wrap securely in foil or other moisture-vapor-proof wrapping and tie in stockinette. Slices of roast meat should be frozen with a protective coating of gravy. Package other foods *after they have cooled.*

Creamed dishes: If cream sauces and gravies separate after freezing, beat with a fork or spoon during reheating. Separation is usually caused by the fat-flour combination. For creamed dishes and a la kings, use the fat sparingly when making the sauce.

Name of food	Storage time
Fish dishes	5 to 8 months
Beef and veal stews	6 months
Meat loaf, meat balls, corned-beef hash, Spanish rice	6 months
Roast meats, poultry	6 months
Creamed dishes, chicken a la king	12 months

Cheese Strata

8 slices white bread or toast
¼ cup soft butter or margarine
2 cups (½ pound) diced sharp process American cheese
4 eggs, slightly beaten
2½ cups milk
1 teaspoon salt
¼ teaspoon dry mustard

Butter bread, quarter and slice. Alternate layers of bread and cheese in 11x7x1½-inch baking dish, ending with cheese.

Mix eggs, milk, and seasonings; pour over layers. Cover and refrigerate overnight. Uncover and bake in slow oven (325°) about 50 minutes or till firm. Let stand a few minutes; cut into 6 squares.

Deviled Egg-Ham Casserole

Deviled Eggs:
6 hard-cooked eggs
¼ cup mayonnaise
1 teaspoon prepared mustard
¼ teaspoon salt
Dash pepper
• • •
¼ cup butter or margarine
¼ cup all-purpose flour
2 cups milk
1 cup shredded sharp process American cheese
1 cup diced cooked or canned ham
½ 10-ounce package (about 1 cup) frozen peas, broken apart
½ cup dry bread crumbs
2 tablespoons butter, melted

Deviled Eggs: Halve eggs. Remove yolks; mash with next 4 ingredients; refill whites.

Arrange eggs in ungreased 10x6x1½-inch baking dish. Melt butter; blend in flour. Gradually stir in milk; cook and stir till thick. Stir in cheese, ham and peas. Pour over eggs. Cool. Cover with foil; refrigerate overnight.

Combine crumbs and butter; sprinkle over. Bake in moderate oven (375°) about 45 minutes. Makes 6 servings.

Chicken Strata

8 slices day-old white bread
2 cups diced cooked chicken
½ cup chopped onion
½ cup chopped green pepper
½ cup finely chopped celery
½ cup mayonnaise
¾ teaspoon salt
2 slightly beaten eggs
1½ cups milk
1 can condensed cream of
  mushroom soup
½ cup shredded sharp process cheese

Butter 2 slices bread; cut in ½-inch cubes and set aside. Cut remaining bread in 1-inch cubes; place half of unbuttered cubes in bottom of 8x8x2-inch baking dish.

Combine chicken, vegetables, mayonnaise, salt, dash pepper; spoon over bread cubes. Sprinkle remaining unbuttered cubes over chicken mixture. Combine eggs and milk; pour over all.

Cover and chill 1 hour or overnight. Spoon soup over top. Sprinkle with buttered cubes. Bake in slow oven (325°) 50 minutes or till set. Sprinkle cheese over top last few minutes of baking. Serves 6.

Limas and Franks

1 pound (2½ cups) large dry Limas
2 teaspoons salt
1 8-ounce can (1 cup) seasoned
  tomato sauce
½ cup finely chopped onion
⅓ cup catsup
3 tablespoons brown sugar
2 tablespoons vinegar
1 tablespoon Worcestershire sauce
2 to 3 teaspoons prepared mustard
1 pound (8 to 10) frankfurters
¼ pound sharp process American
  cheese, cut in strips

Rinse beans; add to 1½ quarts boiling water. Cover; simmer till tender, about 1½ hours, adding salt after 1 hour. Drain.

Place beans in 11½x7½x1½-inch baking dish. Combine next 7 ingredients; pour over beans. Cover with foil; refrigerate mixture overnight.

Next day, heat casserole covered for 30 minutes; stir. Slit franks lengthwise, almost to ends. Insert strip of cheese in each; arrange atop beans. Bake uncovered at 375° for 20 to 25 minutes. Serves 6 to 8.

Barbecued Spareribs

3 to 4 pounds spareribs, cut in pieces
1 cup catsup
⅓ cup Worcestershire sauce
1 teaspoon chili powder
1 teaspoon salt
2 dashes bottled hot pepper sauce
1½ cups water

Salt ribs lightly. Place in shallow roasting pan, meaty side up. Roast in very hot oven (450°) 30 minutes.

Combine next 6 ingredients for sauce; bring to a boil and pour over ribs. Lower temperature control to 350°; bake until well done, about 1½ hours. Baste ribs with sauce every 15 minutes. If sauce gets too thick, add more water. Makes 4 servings.

To freeze: Cool barbecued ribs quickly and thoroughly. Wrap in heavy foil. Seal by folding edges over several times and pressing tightly. Freeze at once.

To serve: Fold back foil; top each piece of ribs with a thin slice of onion and a thin slice of unpeeled lemon. Rewrap or place in shallow baking pan and cover. Heat in hot oven (400°) for 30 to 40 minutes.

Cheese-Meat Loaf

1½ pounds ground beef
1½ cups dry bread crumbs
⅔ cup diced process American cheese
1 cup chopped onion
2 tablespoons chopped green pepper
2 teaspoons salt
1 small bay leaf, crushed
Dash thyme
Dash garlic salt
2 beaten eggs
1 8-ounce can (1 cup) seasoned
  tomato sauce

Combine beef, crumbs, cheese, onion, green pepper, and seasonings; mix thoroughly. Add eggs to tomato sauce; blend into meat mixture. Form in 2 loaves. Line 10x6x1½-inch baking dish with heavy foil, leaving long ends. Place meat loaves in dish. Bake at 350° for 1 hour. Cool thoroughly; fold ends of foil together to seal. Remove wrapped meat from dish; freeze.

To serve: Return meat to original baking dish; open foil. Heat in 350° oven about 1½ hours or till hot. Serves 6 to 8.

Pineapple Ham Loaf—extra good

This handsome glazed loaf is bursting with real ham flavor, boasts parade of broiled pineapple slices and cherries—trim *and* accompaniment!

Pineapple Ham Loaf

1 No. 2 can pineapple slices
½ cup brown sugar
1½ pounds smoked ground ham
1 pound ground fresh pork
¾ cup crushed bite-size
    shredded corn biscuits
½ cup chopped onion
1 teaspoon dry mustard
2 beaten eggs
1 cup milk

Drain pineapple. Reserve 2 tablespoons pineapple syrup, add brown sugar, heat and stir till sugar dissolves. Pour into 9½x5x3-inch loaf pan. Combine remaining ingredients thoroughly. Lightly pack over brown-sugar mixture. Refrigerate overnight.

Bake at 350° for 1 hour and 45 minutes to 2 hours or till done. Remove from oven and let stand 10 minutes.

Meanwhile, brush pineapple slices with melted butter, broil 3 inches from heat about 5 minutes. Pour off excess liquid from loaf; invert on serving plate. Arrange pineapple slices with cherries. Serves 8 to 10.

Bran Muffins

Cream 2 tablespoons shortening and 3 tablespoons sugar; add 1 egg and beat well. Stir in ¾ cup milk, then 1 cup bran flakes. Sift together 1 cup sifted all-purpose flour, 2 teaspoons baking powder, and ½ teaspoon salt; stir into bran mixture just till moistened. Fill greased muffin pans ⅔ full. Bake at 425° about 20 minutes. Makes 1 dozen muffins.

Tuna Salad Bake

1 can condensed cream of
  chicken soup
1 cup diced celery
¼ cup finely chopped onion
½ cup salad dressing or mayonnaise
Dash pepper
3 hard-cooked eggs, sliced
1 6½-, 7-, or 9¼-ounce can tuna,
  well drained
2 cups broken potato chips

Combine first 5 ingredients; fold in egg slices and tuna. Pile into 10x6x1½-inch baking dish. Cover; refrigerate overnight.

To serve: Uncover; top with potato chips. Bake at 400° for 30 minutes. Serves 4 to 5.

Tamale Pie

½ cup chopped onion
½ cup chopped green pepper
¾ pound ground beef
2 8-ounce cans (2 cups) seasoned
  tomato sauce
1 12-ounce can (1½ cups) whole
  kernel corn, drained
½ cup chopped pitted ripe olives
1 clove garlic, minced
1 tablespoon sugar
1 teaspoon salt
2 to 3 teaspoons chili powder
Dash pepper
1½ cups shredded process cheese
• • •
Corn-meal Topper:
¾ cup yellow corn meal
½ teaspoon salt
2 cups cold water
1 tablespoon butter or margarine

Cook onion and green pepper in small amount of hot fat till just tender. Add meat, brown lightly; spoon off excess fat. Add next 8 ingredients. Simmer 20 to 25 minutes or till thick. Add cheese; stir till melted. Pour into 10x6x1½-inch baking dish. Cool thoroughly. Cover tightly with foil; freeze.

To serve: Bake covered at 375° for 1 hour and 15 minutes; add Corn-meal Topper and bake 35 to 40 minutes longer or till hot through and top is browned. Serves 6.

Corn-meal Topper: Stir corn meal and the ½ teaspoon salt into cold water. Cook and stir till thick. Add butter; mix well. Spoon over hot meat mixture in narrow strips.

Curried Lamb

Lamb and curry team up to make a tasty dish—

2 pounds lean lamb breast or
  shoulder, cut in 1-inch cubes
2 cups water
1½ teaspoons salt
1 bay leaf
6 whole black peppers
1 medium onion, sliced
1 teaspoon chopped parsley
• • •
¼ cup all-purpose flour
1 to 2 teaspoons curry powder
4 tablespoons cold water
• • •
Hot cooked rice

Brown meat slowly in hot fat; cover meat with 2 cups water. Add salt, bay leaf, whole peppers, onion, and parsley. Cover and cook slowly for 1½ hours or till meat is tender. Remove meat; remove bay leaf and peppers. Measure stock; add water to make 2 cups, if necessary.

Mix flour and curry powder; slowly stir in cold water and blend smooth. Stir into stock; cook and stir till mixture thickens; pour over meat. Cool quickly by floating pan in ice water. Pour into freezer containers; freeze at once.

To serve: Heat curry mixture in heavy saucepan over low heat about 30 minutes, stirring occasionally. Serve over hot cooked rice. Makes 6 to 8 servings.

Surprise Meat Slices

Here's a magic way to use that frozen cooked meat loaf or roast. We'll bet the family will never guess it's a leftover!—

2 tablespoons fine dry bread crumbs
2 tablespoons grated Parmesan cheese
5 ½-inch slices frozen cooked
  meat loaf *or* 5 thin slices
  frozen cooked roast beef
1 egg, beaten

Combine crumbs and cheese. Dip frozen meat slices in egg; coat with cheese-crumb mixture. Cook meat in small amount hot fat over medium heat, turning once. Cook meat loaf 5 to 7 minutes per side, roast beef 2 minutes per side. Serve with catsup or chili sauce. Makes 5 servings.

Plan ahead. Chill or freeze a super salad

24-Hour Salad

1 No. 2 can (2½ cups) pineapple
tidbits
1 1-pound can (2 cups) pitted
white cherries
3 egg yolks
2 tablespoons *each* vinegar and sugar
1 tablespoon butter or margarine
2 medium oranges, pared and diced
2 cups tiny marshmallows or 16
large ones, cut in eighths
1 cup whipping cream, whipped

Drain pineapple, reserving 2 tablespoons syrup. Drain cherries. In top of double boiler, beat egg yolks slightly; add reserved pineapple syrup, the vinegar, sugar, dash salt, and butter. Place over *hot, not boiling* water; cook, stirring constantly, till mixture thickens *slightly* and *barely* coats a spoon (about 12 minutes). Cool to room temperature.

Combine *well-drained* oranges, pineapple, cherries, and the marshmallows. Pour custard over and mix gently. Fold in whipped cream. Pour into serving bowl. Cover and chill 24 hours. Trim with fresh fruits. Makes 6 to 8 servings.

Coconut Fruit Bowl

1 No. 2 can (2½ cups) pineapple
tidbits, drained
1 11-ounce can (1⅓ cups) mandarin
oranges, drained
1 cup Thompson seedless grapes
1 cup tiny marshmallows
1 3½-ounce can (about 1⅓ cups)
flaked coconut
2 cups dairy sour cream
¼ teaspoon salt

Combine fruits, marshmallows, and coconut. Stir in sour cream and salt. Chill overnight. Makes 8 servings.

Cranberry Fluff

Nice to serve as a luncheon salad or dessert, or let it double as both—

2 cups raw cranberries, ground
3 cups tiny marshmallows
¾ cup sugar
• • •
2 cups diced unpared tart apples
½ cup seedless green grapes
½ cup broken California walnuts
¼ teaspoon salt
1 cup whipping cream, whipped

Combine cranberries, marshmallows, and sugar. Cover and chill overnight. Add apples, grapes, walnuts, and salt. Fold in whipped cream. Chill. Turn into a serving bowl, or spoon into individual lettuce cups. Trim with a cluster of green grapes, if desired. Makes 8 to 10 servings.

Pink Artic Freeze

With dainty chicken sandwiches, it's luncheon—

2 3-ounce packages cream cheese
2 tablespoons mayonnaise or salad
dressing
2 tablespoons sugar
1 1-pound can (2 cups) whole
cranberry sauce
1 9-ounce can (1 cup) crushed
pineapple or pineapple tidbits,
drained
½ cup chopped California walnuts
• • •
1 cup whipping cream, whipped

Soften cheese; blend in mayonnaise and sugar. Add fruits and nuts. Fold in whipped cream. Pour into 8½x4½x2½-inch loaf pan. Freeze firm, 6 hours or overnight. To serve, let stand at room temperature about 15 minutes, turn out on lettuce; slice. Makes 8 to 10 servings.

Frozen Fruit Salad

2 3-ounce packages cream cheese
1 cup mayonnaise

. . .

1 No. 2½ can (3½ cups) fruit
  cocktail, well drained
½ cup drained maraschino cherries,
  quartered
2½ cups tiny marshmallows *or*
  24 large marshmallows, cut in pieces

. . .

1 cup whipping cream, whipped
Red food coloring *or* maraschinocherry juice

Soften cream cheese; blend with mayonnaise. Stir in fruits and marshmallows. Fold in whipped cream. Tint with few drops red food coloring or maraschinocherry juice, if desired.

Pour mixture into two 1-quart round ice-cream or freezer containers, or two No. 2½ cans (or use refrigerator trays). Freeze until firm, about 6 hours or overnight.

To serve, let stand out a few minutes, then remove from containers. Cut in slices. Serve atop lettuce leaves. Trim with maraschino cherries (stems on), if you like. Makes 10 to 12 servings.

Frozen Fruit Salad—luscious!

Fruit cocktail, cherries, and marshmallows polka-dot this rich delicious salad-dessert. For pretty slices, freeze in round freezer cartons.

Frosty Mint Cubes

Drain 1 No. 2 can (2½ cups) crushed pineapple, reserving syrup. Soften *2 teaspoons* unflavored gelatin in syrup. Add ½ cup mint jelly and dash salt; heat, stirring constantly, till gelatin dissolves and jelly melts. (If necessary, beat to blend in jelly.)

Add pineapple. Chill till thick, syrupy. Fold in 1 cup whipping cream, whipped. Tint with few drops green food coloring.

Freeze firm in 1-quart refrigerator tray, 6 hours or overnight. Cut in 1-inch cubes. Serve with chilled fresh or canned pears and peaches, fresh berries. Serves 8 to 10.

Day-before desserts

Apple Stick-ups

It's a dandy served warm or cold—

1⅓ cups water
1 cup sugar
6 inches stick cinnamon, broken
4 large tart apples

• • •

¼ cup slivered blanched almonds,
   toasted
Whipping cream, whipped

Combine water, sugar, and stick cinnamon; bring to a boil. Simmer uncovered 5 minutes. Pare and core apples. Place in hot syrup; cover and simmer just until tender (about 12 to 15 minutes). Don't overcook.

Place apples in 10x6x1½-inch baking dish; pour syrup over. Cover, store in refrigerator. Or, serve without chilling.

To serve: Serve apples in sauce dishes, pour syrup over; stud with toasted almonds. Garnish with whipped cream. Makes 4 servings.

Peach Mystery Meringue

5 egg whites
¼ teaspoon salt
1 cup sugar

• • •

6 to 8 canned peach halves, drained
½ cup whipping cream, whipped
Sliced maraschino cherries *or*
   halved strawberries
Coarsely chopped California walnuts

Preheat oven to 450°. Beat egg whites with salt till soft peaks form. Gradually beat in sugar; continue beating to stiff peaks (about 15 minutes).

Spread in well-greased 8x8x2-inch pan. Place in preheated oven and close door; *turn off heat.* Let stand overnight or at least 5 hours before removing from oven.

To serve: Cut meringues in 6 to 8 squares. Place peach half, cut side up, atop each. Spoon whipped cream over. Top with maraschino cherries or strawberries, and chopped nuts. Makes 6 to 8 servings.

Cooky Fruit Freeze

2 dozen chocolate wafers
1 cup whipping cream, whipped
1 tablespoon sugar
1 teaspoon rum flavoring or vanilla
1 No. 2½ can (3½ cups) fruit
   cocktail, drained
1 ripe banana, sliced
½ cup tiny marshmallows
¼ cup chopped California walnuts

Line the bottom and sides of 8x8x2-inch pan with the chocolate wafers.

Combine whipped cream with sugar and rum flavoring. Fold in fruit cocktail, banana, marshmallows, and walnuts. Pile into cooky-lined pan. Freeze firm.

To serve: Remove from freezer ½ hour before serving. Cut in squares. Serves 9.

Chocolate Souffle

Frozen souffle? Yes, indeed. It thaws as it bakes, puffs up light as can be. Flavor's milk chocolate—

⅓ cup light cream
1 3-ounce package cream cheese
½ cup semisweet chocolate pieces

• • •

3 eggs, separated
¼ teaspoon cream of tartar
Dash salt
3 tablespoons sifted
   confectioners' sugar

Blend cream and cream cheese over very low heat. Add chocolate pieces and stir till melted. Remove from heat. Beat egg yolks until thick and lemon-colored. Gradually blend into chocolate mixture.

Beat egg whites with cream of tartar and salt till soft peaks form. Gradually add sugar, beating till stiff peaks form. Fold into chocolate mixture. Fill 5-ounce or 6-ounce custard cups to within ¼ inch of the top. Cover with foil; freeze.

To serve: Remove foil. Bake in slow oven (300°) 45 minutes or till silver knife inserted comes out clean. Serve immediately. Makes 7 or 8 servings.

Chocolate-Ice Cream Roll

    5 egg whites
    ½ teaspoon cream of tartar
    ½ cup sugar
    5 egg yolks
    ½ cup sugar
    ¼ cup sifted all-purpose flour
    3 tablespoons cocoa
    ¼ teaspoon salt
    1 teaspoon vanilla
            •   •   •
    1 quart pink peppermint ice cream
    1 recipe Chocolate Glaze

Beat egg whites and cream of tartar till stiff but not dry. Gradually beat in ½ cup sugar. Beat egg yolks till thick and lemon-colored. Sift ½ cup sugar with flour, cocoa, and salt; fold into yolks till blended; add vanilla. Carefully fold yolk mixture into whites. Line bottom and sides of 15½x 10½x1-inch pan with waxed paper; grease paper lightly. Spread batter evenly in pan. Bake in slow oven (325°) about 25 minutes. Cool 5 minutes; turn onto towel sprinkled with sifted confectioners' sugar. Peel off paper. Trim side crusts. Roll cake with towel; cool. Unroll.

Stir peppermint ice cream just to soften; gently spread on cake. Roll up. Wrap in waxed paper; freeze. Remove waxed paper, spread with Chocolate Glaze; dot with walnuts. Freeze till serving time. Slice.

Chocolate Glaze

    1 6-ounce package (1 cup) semisweet
        chocolate pieces
    1 6-ounce can (⅔ cup)
        evaporated milk

In small saucepan combine chocolate and milk. Cook and stir over low heat till blended and mixture comes to a boil. Lower heat; cook gently, stirring constantly, for 3 to 5 minutes, or till thick. Cool, stirring constantly. Spread over Chocolate-Ice Cream Roll as directed.

Butter Crunch

You can use this two ways—in Crunch Cups or as a topping for ice cream and puddings—

    ½ cup butter or margarine
    1 cup brown sugar
            •   •   •
    2 cups coarsely crushed corn flakes
    1 cup broken California walnuts

In saucepan, melt butter with brown sugar, stirring constantly. Cook over medium heat 2 to 3 minutes. Remove from heat; quickly add corn flakes and nuts. Spread in thin layer on baking sheet. When cool, crumble coarsely.

Use in Crunch Cups, below. Or sprinkle atop pudding or over ice cream.

Simple and so tasty! You'll make these quick desserts often

Crunch Cups: Make 1 recipe Butter Crunch. Sprinkle bottom of paper cups with 1 to 2 tablespoons Butter Crunch. Cover with small scoop of ice cream. Drizzle with chocolate syrup. Repeat layers, end with Crunch. Freeze till firm. Serve in the cups.

Toasty Coconut Sticks: Prepare one package loaf-size cake mix. Bake in 8x8x2-inch pan. Freeze. Cut cake in 4-inch sticks ½ inch thick. Spread one cut surface with soft butter. Sprinkle with coconut. Bake at 350° about 12 minutes or till coconut is toasted.

Index